HEALING HEARTS

A Young Person's Guide to Discovering the Goodness Within

• • • • • • • • •

JOE CAVANAUGH
WRITTEN WITH
KATIE KELLEY DORN

Nantucket Publications
Minnetonka, MN

First Printing Paperback Edition Published in 1995.

Library of Congress Cataloging-in-Publication Data

Cavanaugh, Joe 1958-
      Healing hearts : a young person's guide to discovering the goodness within /
      Joe Cavanaugh, written with Katie Kelley Dorn.
            p.   cm.
      ISBN 0-9640435-0-5 : $10.95
      1. Good and evil–Juvenile literature.   2. Self-evaluation–Juvenile literature.
      3. Conduct of life–Juvenile literature. [1. Self-evaluation. 2. Conduct of life.]
      I. Dorn, Katie Kelley. II. Title.

      BJ1401.C33 1994   158'.1'0835–dc20   94-8444

Cover illustration of heart is original artwork produced by Betsy Walter at age 16. Betsy is now a young artist/illustrator studying at the University of Minnesota and The Minneapolis College of Art & Design. She currently lives in Hastings, MN with her turtle, Dexter.

Layout and other illustrations by Wendy Wright, *wrighters, ink.,* St. Paul, MN.

Printed in the United States of America.

Contents

Dedication   1

Part One:
OUR HURTING HEARTS   3

Part Two:
SEEING INSIDE OURSELVES   11

Part Three:
FINDING THE GOODNESS IN OTHERS   33

Close   49

Dedication

One of my heroes in life was a tall, skinny eighteen-year-old boy named Spenser Somers. Spenser's spirit and humor were legendary to those who knew him. Rarely a day went by when a Spenserism (a bit of humor or wisdom from Spenser) wasn't shared with others.

Spenser wore a baseball cap all the time to cover his bald head which was the result of his ongoing battle with chemotherapy. Spenser had a wisdom that only a young person facing his mortality could have. Young, wise people are as rare as old, passionate people. Our world needs more of both.

Sitting at a restaurant one day, he and I were laughing and sharing stories of life. It was then that Spenser told me about a summer trip he took with his church youth group to Colorado.

"Everyone was trying to give me all the answers," he said, "Here I am facing life and death, and everyone was trying to give me answers. I'm not looking for answers. I'm just looking for someone to help me struggle through the questions."

Alas, such was the wisdom and depth of Spenser.

If I could sum up this book in a few words, it would be that its purpose is not to give you all the answers. Its purpose is to help you struggle through the questions. Questions about seeing inside yourself and others more clearly.

When I think of my friend Spenser, I am grateful that even though his life was cut short by cancer, his courageous battle with the great questions of life have showed me how to struggle with many of life's questions.

My hope is that the following chapters will do the same for you. Whether you work through the questions in this book alone, with your family, or with a group of friends, hopefully it will help you to see yourself and others better.

I know that it would have been Spenser's hope, too. That is why I dedicate this book to his memory.

• • • • • • • • • • •

Part One

OUR HURTING HEARTS

As humans, we have a great capacity to love and to be loved. But for many of us, our capacity to give and to receive that love becomes limited because we come to the relationships in our lives with hurting hearts.

I'm working with teenagers across the country, and I'm saddened by how so many hearts are hurting from years of bites and stings along life's path. Each time we were lonely, or someone called us a name, or told us that we didn't matter, it hurt a little more. As we began to believe the negative and hurtful things that happened, it stung and ached. So to stop the pain, we built a wall. These walls protected our hearts because we didn't want to feel lonely, or ashamed, or like a nobody. We didn't want to hurt anymore.

We're smart, too. Without even knowing it, we started building our walls at a very young age. It is our self-preservation instinct.

But what we don't realize as we're slowly constructing walls to block out the pain is that the walls also block out the goodness and joy in our lives. The walls around our hearts stop us from seeing and from feeling the good things that people tell us or see in us, or that we used to see in ourselves. And thus the hurt grows deeper.

We have heard it a million times, "It's what's on the inside that counts." But do we believe it? Can we look deep inside ourselves, beyond the walls that block our hurts, and see the goodness that is deep within us and believe it wholeheartedly? Finding our goodness within is what makes us believe in ourselves. It makes us confident. It gives us joy.

Can we look inside others and see beyond their skin color, beyond their clothes, beyond their grades, and beyond their label? A jock. A burn-out. A loner. A brain.

When we build a wall that blocks us from seeing the goodness in ourselves, it also limits our ability to truly see the goodness in others. In high school I was too concerned with where I fit in and how I could be liked by others. Do people like me? A better question would have been, do I like myself? Do I even see myself when I look inside?

Larry the Lawnchair Man

A number of years ago there was a story in the newspaper about a man named Larry. Larry lived by the Los Angeles airport and would sit in his lawnchair in his backyard every day and watch the planes take off and land. He loved to watch the planes, and he wished he could get a better view of the planes as they flew by so that he could really see them. Even if only 40 feet higher, he knew that he could then enjoy his hobby of watching planes all the more.

So Larry got an idea. He got together some friends to help him inflate four weather balloons with helium. With the help of his friends, they tied all of the four weather balloons to his lawnchair. And sure enough, up went Larry the Lawnchair Man strapped in his lawnchair. Higher and higher. He made it to 40 feet. But he didn't stop there. Nor did he stop at 100 feet. Nor 500. Nor 1,000. Larry the Lawnchair man finally stopped at 10,000 feet in the air.

The Los Angeles airport traffic controllers were baffled. What was this UFO in their flight pattern? They had to re-route air traffic until Larry floated down. Can you imagine what the pilot from Northwest Airlines Flight 520 said as he flew by? "Oh my, God! Traffic control! Traffic control! There's a man in a lawnchair up here…and I think that he's sipping a Slurpee!"

Soon the authorities were gathered in Larry's backyard. The police. The fire department. The paramedics. The reporters. The television cameras. All were waiting for Larry the Lawnchair Man as he slowly floated down.

When he reached the ground, he was barraged by reporters. There were three questions they wanted to ask Larry.

The first, "Were you scared?"

"Yes," answered Larry as he shook his head up and down.

The second, "Would you ever do it again?"

"No," as he shook his head side to side.

Finally, "Why? Why did you do it?"

And what did Larry say?

"Well, you just can't sit there…not if you want to see."

That story got national attention because people are intrigued by the bizarre. But it got my attention for a different reason.

Sometimes we just can't sit there…not if we want to see. We've got to take some risks so that we can see ourselves and grow. For it is only when we can break down our self-built walls and see beyond the negatives and the pain that we can discover our goodness inside. The goodness that has always been inside each of us, hiding beyond the wall of a hurting heart.

My hope is that the pages in this book encourage you to tie on some weather balloons to the "chair" in which you are sitting. If you are going to see and grow, in Larry's words, "You can't just sit there."

This book is about seeing what's on the inside. Beyond what we don't like. Beyond the hurts and pains. Those hurts and pains are there, but there is so much more for us to see when we look inside ourselves.

It is about being brave enough to see inside ourselves and others.

And when we look deep inside ourselves, we learn to see beyond the things we don't like and find the goodness that is often unseen. Then we can accept ourselves not for what we accomplish, or what we look like, or what others think of us, but just for who we are.

And once we accept ourselves and find that goodness, we can begin to believe in the love that our family and friends have for us. And we begin to feel like we're floating 10,000 feet in the air, sitting in our lawnchair and sipping a Slurpee.

It's then that we can feel good enough about ourselves to let some-one look deep into our eyes. And that is where friendship is born.

And each and every time a friendship is born, hearts are healed.

• • • • • • • • • • • •

Journal Entry One

Reread the story of Larry the Lawnchair Man. Being on the ground held Larry back from seeing better. What things in your life hold you back from seeing yourself? List 3-5 things and tell how they hold you back.

_____

_____

_____

_____

_____

_____

Who in your life holds you back from seeing the goodness inside yourself and why?

_____

_____

_____

_____

_____

_____

_____

_____

_____

_____

Like Larry, do you ever fantasize about getting away from what holds you back from seeing better? Where do you dream of going, or what do you dream of doing, that takes you 10,000 feet in the air so that you can really be free from your wall and see inside yourself? List 5-7 things you dream of doing or having in your life?

_____

_____

_____

_____

_____

_____

_____

_____

_____

_____

_____

_____

_____

_____

_____

_____

What specific things do you need to do to realize those dreams? What "balloons" can you bring with you each day to help you get away, to reach your dreams, to see the goodness you have? Is it time alone? Is it time with a special friend that you can really talk to? Is it a hobby or interest that you enjoy? List 3-4 things that you need to do for yourself or need to risk that will help you live and see better?

_____

_____

_____

_____

_____

_____

_____

_____

_____

_____

_____

_____

_____

_____

_____

_____

_____

• • • • • • • • • • •

Part Two

SEEING INSIDE OURSELVES

Being a short boy was not the way it was supposed to be. If only I could be just three inches taller then everything would be all right! Even two inches, even one inch!

But there I was, standing 5' 6" tall or rather 5' 6" short, and that was with big heels. Being tall seemed a criterion in that all-important category of what's important as a teenager.

"God, please make me cool…"

And God's response was, "Joe, there are some things that even I cannot do."

As a 7th grader I felt like a newborn in Nikes. As a 10th grader, I felt like a 7th grader who shaved.

The Softball Throw

I sighed when my mom told me I had to get up for school. It was Thursday, and on Thursday in gym class we had the softball throw. The only thing worse than the softball throw for us short guys was the memory of the punt, pass, and kick competition in third grade. You see, being short meant you really couldn't throw the softball very far. Maybe it had to do with Newtonian physics or something. But as hard as us short guys tried, we rarely measured our softball success in anything more than a few yards.

Bruce was the greatest athlete at South View Junior High. You know, the kind of guy who does shave in seventh grade.

It was time. "Bruce!" the gym teacher bellowed. "Show us how to throw the softball."

"Yes, coach," Bruce's baritone voice said with the utmost confidence.

And he threw, or rather he launched the ball far into the sky. Trees lost their leaves, roofs blew off, the gym teacher's toupee flew off as the softball seemed to circle the globe at least twice, and still the ball landed near the house across the street from school.

"Wow!" everyone watching sighed. "Bruce is cool."

Now the moment had come. It was my turn.

"Joe, your turn for the softball throw."

All I could do in my fashionable gym uniform was to attempt to lift the ball up. "Will somebody help me pick up the ball please? It's so heavy…heavy it is…"

I felt like a powerless Yoda. And with a mighty roar that sounded more like a squeak, I threw the ball. I would have had better luck throwing a feather. And everyone there was watching. I could have sworn I heard, "Joe's a geek." And worst of all my dream girl, Marsha, was watching.

I shrunk a little bit that day. Not my body. I had no height to spare.

But my heart. It seemed to shrivel up a little bit that day. So did my adolescent self-esteem.

Why? Because I couldn't throw a rubberized ball wrapped in leather very far.

Or rather because I saw the softball throws in life as more important than the inside parts of me. Because I didn't look inside myself and see the good things.

Why? Because if I did try to look at myself, all that glared at me were the unimportant things on the outside. Mostly things I didn't like. And I built a little more of my wall that day to ease the pain.

How tall I was. How far I could throw the softball. What grade I got in history.

Who cared if I got an "F" in Life. It was more important to get an "A" in history. It's so easy to do. We become obsessed with getting the medal in track, the trophy in basketball, or the lead part in the musical because that is what we believe is most important in life. We think our "15 minutes" of fame will satisfy our craving to feel at peace in life and will heal the hurts inside our hearts.

We take the things that are on the outside and make them the focus of life itself. And in doing so, we begin to lose sight of what is truly important. The importance of winning trophies for our character and the standing ovations for our integrity.

I Was in Love With Marsha Brady

My heart shriveled up a little bit that day on the gym field because I saw myself through everyone else's eyes, especially Marsha's. I felt her eyes upon me that Thursday on the gym field, dressed in my gym fatigues by Jordache, as I hurled the ball an unprecedented three yards.

You see, Marsha was my dream girl. We all have dream dates, the one you hope will like you. And you hope they dream about you the way you dream about them.

Yes, Marsha Brady was my dream date. But Marsha seemed to only like the tall, dark, and handsome guys. Being short, I only had a chance for two out of three.

Two years later in high school, Marsha was still my desired "Juliet." Two of my friends, Dave and Mike, somehow convinced me that Marsha wanted to go with me to the Homecoming Dance. Perhaps it was my active imagination, or perhaps I thought she was different and could look beyond the insecurities I wore on my sleeve. Mom always told me that the right person would see beyond my being short or not throwing the softball far enough. Mothers always say such noble things.

So I believed my mom and I believed Marsha was the right person for me. Which meant she could see beyond those things, too, and like me for me.

I decided to ask her during lunch. I was going to get up my nerve and invite her to the dance. She usually sat with her friends at a table that was two down from ours. Little did I know that Mike and Dave had told half of the lunchroom that I was going to ask Marsha to the dance. They had it all planned out. As I asked her to the Homecoming Dance, everyone would do the wave.

"Marsha?"

"Yeh…" she said in the sweetest, softest voice a teenage boy could ever imagine.

"Would you like to go the the homecoming dance with me?" My words came out sounding more like a seal than a man of 16 years.

And as I asked, the entire room started doing the wave. I realized my fear.

I was mortified. I wanted to crawl under the lunch table and hide in the spilled chow mein while staring up at the dried gum under the tabletop. I wanted to escape so it would all go away, like a bad dream.

Yet Marsha surprised me. She was unphased by the explosion of laughter in the cafeteria. Maybe my mom was right. Maybe this girl could see beyond….

"Thanks for asking me to the dance, Joe. That's sweet. You are so nice."

"Ugh!" I thought. "Here it comes."

"And I really like you." And then came that dreaded phrase, "But just

<u>as a friend</u>." Later I found out she was already going to the dance with her boyfriend who graduated last year (a college freshman).

"Just as a friend." The dreaded words for a 5'6" 16-year-old.

Boom! Mom was wrong. They all saw me like I saw myself. Like a Nobody. And I felt myself building another layer of bricks around my heart.

"You mean I'm a Nobody, don't you."

"No, Joe, you're not a nobody…" And then she would say the word that should be struck from all dictionary's from Webster's to Heritage.

"You're not a nobody, Joe, you're…*cute*."

Cute is the death knell for any male. Why not just say, "You shop at Geeks-R-Us?" You see, I believed that being a short, cute boy in high school who couldn't throw the softball meant that I was a Nobody. Or so I thought.

It seemed that in high school there was something terribly wrong with being "just a friend." All I could hear was her saying no to the dance…and no to me…who was just a big, or rather little, Nobody.

• • • • • • • • • • •

Journal Entry Two

Can you remember a time when something or someone made you feel like a Nobody? Think back and remember. Describe the incident and how you felt about yourself at that time.

_____

_____

_____

_____

_____

_____

_____

_____

_____

_____

_____

_____

_____

_____

_____

_____

_____

_____

_____

_____

Sometimes the hurt of a situation can paralyze us. But when you look back, you can learn something positive from the situation that will help you break down your wall a little bit. Think back to a time you felt like a "Nobody." Looking back at it now, was there something positive or good that you can learn from your experience?

_____

_____

_____

_____

_____

_____

_____

_____

_____

_____

_____

_____

_____

_____

_____

_____

_____

_____

_____

Go back to that day you felt like a Nobody. Write a letter to yourself. Be kind and compassionate as you try to uplift the hurt part of you. (Hint: Pretend you are a friend trying to heal your hurt a little bit.)

Dear _____(your name here),

_____

_____

_____

_____

_____

_____

_____

_____

_____

_____

_____

_____

_____

_____

_____

_____

_____

_____

_____

Sticks and Stones

We remember the hurts of our lives. The feelings of humiliation as people do the wave and shout our name in the lunchrooms of life. We stuff the hurtful memories behind the wall around our hearts and let it burden us.

We remember. We especially remember the crummy stuff. The ugly things that people tell us. We remember and start to believe.

On the playground as a little kid, I was called "Caviar"…tiny fish eggs …or "Shrimp." I had already begun building the wall around my heart to protect myself from being hurt by those names. So I would laugh instead. But often it wasn't all that funny.

I'd repeat those word my mom taught me, "Sticks and stones may break my bones, but names will never hurt me."

"Sticks and stones may break my bones, but names will never hurt me."

How untrue that is. I knew it then. And I'm sure of it now.

The truth is more like "Sticks and stones may break my bones, but names are what really hurt me."

Names hurt to the core. Sticks and stones may bruise me, but those bruises heal. They go away in a few short days. The bruises on our hearts from name-calling stick like Elmer's glue.

Each and every cruel word breaks a heart a little bit. Sadly, playgrounds and hallways have become breeding grounds for words that scar and hurt people. I'm not sure about others, but I would rather have a stick thrown at me any day – except a sharp-pointed one. I'd forget that short-lived pain. But painful words never go away. Years later they still can sting.

97 vs. 3

And the more times I was hurt, the bigger the wall to protect my heart grew. And the bigger the wall, the harder it was for me to see the goodness inside myself. All I could see was the crummy stuff. The things I didn't like.

One day in ninth grade our math teacher, Mrs. Larson, handed back our mid-term exams. I got an 86. The person next to me got a 97 (97 right, 3 wrong).

His response was, "Three wrong! Three wrong! I'm so stupid, how could I get three wrong?"

"Mrs. Larson," this grade curve champion said as he raised his hand, "I think you should look at my work on problem #15 again. It could be interpreted differently if you look at my work…"

Often we are unable to see the 97 right. All we see is the 3 wrong.

It becomes like that in many areas of our lives. The more we just see the crummy stuff, the 3% that's wrong, the harder it is for us to see the 97% that's right in our life.

I'm not saying that the 3 wrong isn't there, but too often we, and others, just focus on the 3. We see the faults in others, all the things we don't like.

We look in the mirror as we get ready for school and say, "Three wrong." We need to have something or someone in the mirror shout, "Hey, what about the 97 right!"

As I've examined my life over the years, and worked with teenagers across the country, I've seen a pattern. A scary pattern.

We believe too many messages we hear. And we especially believe the crummy stuff. If you tell me something good, I'll forget it by tomorrow. But tell me something bad and I'll remember it for years. A compliment lasts a minute, a criticism lasts a lifetime.

Sticks and stones may break my bones, but names are what really hurt me.

Between the "perfect" physical standards set by models and sports heroes in the media; the lotions and potions that are advertised telling us we need to look better, feel better, and be better; the grades we get in school that tell us if we've passed or failed; the messages we get from those in control that tell us to "be quiet and sit still;" it's no wonder it's hard to believe that we are good. It's easy to compare ourselves to the unreachable standards set by others and count all the ways we don't measure up. To see what we don't like about ourselves and what we think others don't like about us.

Yet, that's all on the outside. It's not who or what we are.

Journal Entry Three

What were some of the "words" you were called on the playground?

_____

_____

_____

What were some of the "words" you called others on the playground?

_____

_____

_____

Do those memories stick with you today? Why or why not?

_____

_____

_____

Write down the three things you think are "wrong" or you don't like about yourself. Do this quickly in 10 words or less for each one.

1. _____

2. _____

3. _____

Now, write down 10 things you *do* like about yourself for each of the 3 things you *don't* like about yourself. You'll end up with a list of 30 things you like about yourself, compared to 3 things you don't like. This could be your first step to finding the 97% right or good about yourself. If you run into trouble finding 30 things you like about yourself, look at old yearbook entries from friends, old letters, old birthday cards, or talk to a parent or best friend and have them help you find the 97% right and good in yourself compared to just the 3% wrong.

1. _____
2. _____
3. _____
4. _____
5. _____
6. _____
7. _____
8. _____
9. _____
10. _____
11. _____
12. _____
13. _____
14. _____
15. _____

16. _____
17. _____
18. _____
19. _____
20. _____
21. _____
22. _____
23. _____
24. _____
25. _____
26. _____
27. _____
28. _____
29. _____
30. _____

Pick out your 5 favorite things you like about yourself and write them on a piece of paper. Tape it on the mirror in your bedroom or next to your bed where you can read it everyday.

I am

I have a good friend, Lynn, who teaches 7th grade in the Twin Cities. During the first week of school, she asks her students to answer five questions so she can get to know them better. The questions are actually statements each student needs to complete:

I am:_____

I am:_____

I am:_____

I am:_____

I am:_____

One year she let me read through the statements from her class to get some insight into how 7th graders today feel about themselves. The first one I read was from a 7th grade girl who obviously had a pretty good self-concept and a good sense of humor. It read:

1. I am good looking
2. I am a good athlete
3. I am highly intelligent
4. I am very popular
5. I am somewhat conceited

I smiled to myself. "Maybe kids today have a better self-concept than when I was in 7th grade." But then I read on through the stack. And they got worse. And worse. And worse.

About halfway through the stack I came to one essay from a student that really disturbed me. It troubled me for days after I read it:

I am _____(left blank)
I am _____(left blank)
I am _____(left blank)
I am _____(left blank)
I am Nothing

What had this young 7th grader been told that made him believe he was a nothing. Had his parents told him, "You are a good-for-nothing so and so…" Or had his best friend dropped him for a "cooler group" and made him feel like a Nothing? Or had he fallen through the cracks at school? Was he ignored like a Nothing? Was he abused? Was he at risk?

It troubled me for days. And it brought me back 20 years. I began to remember how easy it is to believe the messages that people give us. Those negative messages begin to brutalize us and paralyze us from seeing the good in ourselves. How easy it is to look at ourselves and not be able to see beyond that which we don't like. All we can see is what's wrong.

It's hard to whittle down a stone wall around our heart that we've built over years and years. But the best way to chisel away at that wall is to begin to look inside ourselves. To see, to accept, and to believe. To believe that deep beyond the wall we've built to protect our heart is the goodness that was there the day we were born. Before anybody or anything told us we were a nobody.

We have to believe that goodness is there even if we don't feel like it's there. At times when I was in high school, I felt shorter than I was. I wasn't a star athlete. I never dated Marsha Brady. And my Dad, in his orange plaid pants and brown stripped shirt, would come to school, find me in the hallway and say, "Here's your chicken salad sandwich, Joe. You forgot it at home. I put a little of the vanilla pudding you like so much in there, the kind that comes with the spoon that changes color." And everyone would laugh, or so it seemed, and I thought I would die. All I could see was the 3% that was wrong in my life.

But as years went by, I realized that I couldn't take the unimportant and make it all important. I couldn't take my failings and what I didn't like about myself, or what I didn't achieve, and make them all of who I was. I learned that I was good simply because I am. That's it. No other reason. That I was created unlike any other person on this earth. That there was goodness within me just like any other person. That I had talents, warmth, and goodness that were unique to me alone.

And that by finding that uniqueness, and believing in that instead of believing in the just the crummy stuff, I found more joy. Like Larry the Lawnchair Man, I started to feel like I was really seeing all of me for the first time. That I was 10,000 feet up in the sky. I even started to appreciate my dad's orange plaid pants.

It's there for all of us to find. Perhaps we need to take a risk and tie on some weather balloons to find it. My hope is that through this book, you will take the time to find your goodness again. To see the 97 and not just the 3.

In Journal Entry 4, take your time to attach your balloons. Think it through and try to re-find your goodness. When you're done with your journal entry, read it over each day until you start feeling your wall break down and begin to see your goodness.

Journal Entry Four

Complete the five "I am" essay statements, but complete them with the goodness that's deep within you that makes you unique and special. The talents, attributes, and gifts that you have that make you a unique creation. Not because of what you do or how you do it, simply because you are. Perhaps it is "I like animals" or "I'm kind to others" or "I'm a good listener." Then give an example in the past week when you used that goodness and how it made you feel. (Example: "I'm a good listener. This week a friend of mine was feeling really down about an argument with her sister. I listened to her for two hours one night as she worked out a way to make up with her sister. I felt really good.")

I am:_____

_____

_____

_____

_____

I am:_____

_____

_____

_____

I am:_____

_____

_____

_____

_____

I am:_____

_____

_____

_____

_____

I am:_____

_____

_____

_____

_____

Write these down on a smaller piece of paper and carry them with you in your wallet or purse everyday. Whenever you're feeling the wall go up around your heart or you start believing the crummy stuff the world tells you, pull out your "I am" list and read it five times.

Finding Our Goodness Within

As you travel on your journey to break down the wall around your heart, I hope that you will find your goodness within. It is a lifelong journey and it is a great adventure.

And my hope is that you'll start to believe that you are unique and special. And that belief will be something you can hold onto so that the hurts and pains of life won't take away the goodness. It's not only what you do that defines who you are. You are and always will be unique, gifted, and talented just because you are you.

There will always be people and circumstances that will focus on the 3%. Grades, getting cut from a team, breaking up with a girl or boyfriend, bad softball throws, embarrassing moments in the cafeteria. And the list gets longer as you get older. That's why we need to begin the journey as soon as possible. Because if we've accepted ourselves and found our goodness, the 3% no longer tears us down, but instead, challenges us to grow.

Pull out your "I am" list every time you start believing that those negative experiences or statements define who you are. Don't let them take away the goodness that you've found. Learn from them and move on. But don't hold on to the negative messages. Hold on to the positive, the parts that reinforce who you are. The 97%.

Believing in yourself and your goodness allows you to live out that goodness. And that is a very freeing, joyful way to live. Much better than hiding yourself and your heart behind a wall.

And the more you find and live out your goodness, the more people will begin to see it in you. It is then that your goodness starts to come full-circle.

Continuing Your Journey

This journey is your own. It will be different for each person. But one thing I know from working with groups across the country, it's an ongoing journey. It never ends.

My hope is that this book can be a map for your journey. Look inside yourself. Look beyond the wall you've built and really, really see. Not just the 3%, but maybe for the first time your 97%. See your goodness. And begin to heal your heart.

• • • • • • • • • • •

FINDING THE GOODNESS IN OTHERS

I remember very well the first day I got glasses. I was in third grade and I was driving home. Actually, being only a third grader, I wasn't driving…my mom was driving. I looked out the window and for the first time in my life saw that trees had leaves. I could see things that I never thought were there.

Oftentimes we don't see things right. Until someone or something or some event gives us "glasses" to see better. When we use our hearts to see better, we begin to accept ourselves more. We begin to feel stronger and freer. We begin to see the internal goodness in ourselves and in others. Labels become less important, what people "do" becomes less important than who they are. When you see better, you see inside people's eyes and see their soul.

One of those people who has helped me see better was a high school friend of mine who was on the wrestling team with me, as well as on a peer helping staff that did outreach work to our fellow high school students. His name was Jim.

Jim

Jim was challenged in life because he was blind. He memorized the hallways, memorized his walk to school, memorized the running track so he could work out. He was simply amazing, an inspiration to all of us who knew him.

One day Jim and I were at a local restaurant, and it was unknown territory for him. He had to feel his way as he made his way to the restroom.

People stared. People do that quite naturally. I've done it, you've done it, we've all done it. When someone is different, we stare. And on this particular day, I found myself getting angry. I wanted to shout at all the staring people, "What are all of you staring at? You think he is blind? He's not the blind one, we're the blind ones. Yeh, Jim can't see…he can't see clothing styles, body shapes, skin colors, but Jim sees better than any of us. He sees people with his heart! He's not blinded by his eyes!"

Jim saw the inside of people, not the outside. He cared about me and was my friend; not for my outside, but for my inside. He got to know who I really was.

It's like that Grateful Dead song, sometimes you have to have "a blind man take you by the hand and say, 'Don't you see?'" He did that for me. He touched my heart and helped me to see better. He has inspired me to do that with others.

Thank God for the Jims in our lives. The people who help us see better. Too often we look in the mirror and see ourselves as we saw our last math test, 3 wrong! Too often our blindness just sees the areas that need growth, not how far we have come. We only see the extra pound, the scar, the fault. We become blinded to all that is good. We see our curses and forget our blessings whether in our families, friends, schools, ourselves.

Then, tragically, we begin to use what is left of our eyes to look at people. We make people into objects. We see people in our culture degraded in the hallways, sexually harassing names like "slut" or "faggot" thrown at them, racial slurs, children teased about their bodies, or women made into paper on the magazine racks of pornography.

Thank God for the other Jims of the world who teach us how to see better, to not look <u>at</u> but to look <u>in</u>.

The eyes are the windows to our souls. If you want to see if someone has been loved or abused in life, look in their eyes. Perhaps that is one of the great needs of all of us, to have someone look in our eyes and not at us.

When was the last time another person looked <u>in</u> you and not <u>at</u> you?

When we look <u>at</u> people in our homes or in our school hallways, we make them into objects, thereby stripping them of their humanity. And when we no longer see the humanity in others, we gain the capacity to devalue anything or anyone, even ourselves.

Then it becomes easy to shove someone unpopular into a locker and laugh, or take advantage of someone sexually on a date, or mock a homeless person lying on the street. When we look at people and make them into objects, then it doesn't matter any more what happens to them. A double tragedy occurs: they become unimportant, and we become blind to what is truly important in life.

Perhaps it's because we would rather look at a Nintendo screen than look inside someone's eyes. In the words of one of my mentors in life, "Our bellies are full but our spirits are empty."

• • • • • • • • • • • •

Journal Entry Six

List some examples where you see people (individuals or groups) being made into objects.

_____

_____

_____

_____

_____

_____

Where in your life are you "blind?" In what areas of your life are you preoccupied with the unimportant "outside" stuff? List 3-5 outside things that have blinded you. How can you work on those things to help you see better? (Example: Being in "your group" blinded you from being friends with someone because of how they dressed or looked.)

_____

_____

_____

_____

_____

_____

_____

_____

_____

Who have you judged recently in your life by looking <u>at</u> and not <u>in</u>? List some people you have done this to recently. (Example: I've always looked <u>at</u> not <u>in</u> my mother. I just expect her to work all day and come home and cook and do my laundry. I never looked at her as a person with feelings and needs, too. I'm going to try to see her as a person and recognize her feelings.)

_____

_____

_____

_____

_____

_____

_____

_____

_____

_____

_____

_____

_____

_____

_____

_____

_____

_____

"Our bellies are full, but our spirits are empty." It strikes me as I travel around the country working with young people that many times it is the seemingly "all-together" kids who have an empty spirit. They may have filled their bellies with all the "outside" stuff… the right clothes, the right looks, the right friends, the right teams, even the right words. But in my conversations with them, they tell me they feel empty. Inside they still hurt. All they see is the 3 wrong.

But what strikes me even more is that it is often those kids that the world defines with empty bellies that are truly rich in spirit. It seems that when their outsides are stripped away, these young people see our insides and show us our goodness. That is certainly true with Charlie.

Charlie

Charlie was a nine-year-old like any other until a fire destroyed his home and covered most of his body with third degree burns. Those of us who know burn victims, or the pain and anguish they must go through in the burn treatment centers, know the courage and strength they must have to survive the ordeal. Whether it's soaking in bathtubs of antibiotic solutions to protect against infection or the torturous pain of changing bandages, the nurses and doctors see the courage of the great fighters for life. Charlie wore splints between his fingers to keep the skin from webbing together. He wore a tight plastic mask on his face, not to hide his ugly scars, but to keep his eyes and mouth from sealing shut as his body slowly healed.

After six months Charlie could walk. He would get up and walk around the burn unit and encourage others who were new to the battle for life. The chances of Charlie looking good in a pair of designer jeans again were unlikely, but he was doing much more than winning a modeling contest, he was winning a battle for life itself. He was loving others and learning to be loved.

After two years Charlie went back to his elementary school. You can imagine the first day. People tend to avoid those who are different. Different body shapes, skin colors, clothing styles, etc. tend to invoke fear which destroys love.

The first lunch he was sitting at a table by himself (even the surrounding tables were empty). People tend to avoid those who are special and unique. Everyone was sitting at their own tables, the super-cool group (or rather the group that thought they were super cool), the not cool-group, the medium-cool group. It always amazes me how people in school lunchrooms have their reserved tables, keeping others away by threatening them with their hoagie buns.

One girl named Lisa (I don't know what group she was in) got up and walked across the lunchroom. Standing next to Charlie, she looked into his eyes. When you look into someone's eyes you no longer see the outside body shapes, skin colors, or clothing styles. You see the person.

She said, "Hi, my name is Lisa. What's yours?"

Charlie, his voice damaged from the fire, spoke in a raspy voice, "My name is Charlie."

Lisa said, "Hi Charlie, I want to be your friend."

Charlie looked into Lisa's eyes and responded, "Do you see all these other people, they might not like me now, but wait until they get to know me…wait until they get to know me."

Charlie and Lisa are those people who see what is really important in life. They are the people in our lives who remind us of the important lesson of seeing beyond the outside. They teach us to look beyond. To look into someone's eyes and see their inside, to see the real person and the goodness that rests inside. That is what heart healers do. And it's contagious.

• • • • • • • • • • •

Journal Entry Seven

Who in the past year has looked into your eyes and helped you to see the goodness inside of you? Describe what they did to show you.

_____

_____

_____

_____

_____

_____

_____

_____

_____

Who in your whole life has looked into your eyes and helped you to see the goodness inside of you? Describe what they did to show you.

_____

_____

_____

_____

_____

_____

_____

_____

_____

List some of the characteristics of these people. Are they heart healers? What did they teach you?

_____

_____

_____

_____

_____

_____

_____

_____

_____

_____

_____

_____

_____

_____

_____

_____

_____

_____

_____

_____

_____

_____

The Campfire

I work at a small company called Youth Frontiers which works with schools around the country. We do retreat programs for schools on important values and building community within the school. Many times we end the retreats with a campfire and have students share thoughts of what they would like their school community to be like. These "campfires" are probably the most powerful sharing experiences I have ever witnessed with people of any age. Teachers have often said that they have never seen such wonder and compassion among students in their school. Sometimes the effect fades quickly, yet rarely do the students forget the experience of mutual care and respect.

A few years ago, during a campfire for a high school freshman class retreat, I experienced that wonder while observing the interaction between two boys, James and David. James was a small, tough boy who hadn't participated in the discussions all day, except for an occasional wisecrack while I was talking or a holler to someone "cool" across the room. In fact, he spent most of the day in the back of the room, arms folded across his leather jacket, and chair leaning against the wall.

The other boy, David, sat in the corner of the room. His head was down, and he spent most of the retreat alone. He never looked up or spoke all day.

We ended the retreat that day like we usually do, with everybody sitting around the campfire made of candles with school colors. James got up and walked to the "campfire" at the center of the room. And as James picked up the microphone in front of 200 of his peers, he spoke to that one particular boy who seemed to be somewhat of a loner. "David," James said. "For the past year I have made fun of you and beat you up in the halls. My friends encouraged me as I did it to you. They laughed. I laughed. We thought it was a joke."

James paused and then said, "I want you to know that I am not going to do that anymore." He then turned to the rest of the class and said, "I want all of you to remind me of this if I am mean to David in the future."

With that, James put down the microphone and walked back to his place in the circle and sat down. David never responded with anything more than a nod, but I am confident that James had healed David's heart a little bit that day. Rarely have I seen such courage, honesty, or compassion from a teenager or even an adult.

Someone recently told me James dropped out of school. I believe that school experienced a great loss the day James left. I could tell that he was from a tough crowd and probably caused many a headache for teachers and principal, but that type of courage is what is needed to begin to heal the hearts of people in our homes, schools, hallways, neighborhood streets, and communities.

People like James remind us what it means to stop looking at people and to start looking in people. To start treating one another as human beings and not objects that can be discarded as some do with note-book paper on the floors of our school halls. We don't have to dehumanize people. As a wise person once said, "Just because we can't all be friends, that doesn't mean we have to be enemies."

James might not have been the homecoming king, basketball captain, youth-group regular, or student council member, but he was showing his 97 that day. His toughness disappeared in the light of the campfire. In the words of a senior named Amy, "No one is ever ugly by campfire light." Great wisdom from another teenager who shows us how to see better. Perhaps we should exchange the fluorescent spotlights in our school hallways for campfire light. By campfire light you can see the 97. The 3 is still there but the 97 is so much easier to focus on. Maybe that's why romantics use candles at dinner.

"No one is ever ugly by campfire light."

• • • • • • • • • • •

Journal Entry Eight

Who in your life have you looked in not at, and helped them to see the goodness inside of themselves?

_____

_____

_____

_____

_____

_____

_____

_____

_____

_____

_____

_____

_____

_____

_____

_____

_____

_____

_____

Who is one person in your home or school whom you think needs a heart healer to look into his/her eyes?

_____

_____

_____

List 3-5 simple ways you can be a heart healer to that person (Example: Say "hi," send a note, sit with him/her at the game, etc.)

_____

_____

_____

_____

_____

_____

_____

_____

_____

_____

_____

_____

_____

_____

_____

• • • • • • • • • • •

Close
• • • • • • • • • • •

To me, one of the greatest people to ever live was my grandma. It is rare to find passionate old people, but she was one.

Even though she lived a full life of 86 years and touched the hearts of all the people she came in contact with, she still died too soon. Not enough people got to know her. If you ever met a 4'11" Italian woman named Theresa Saiya, you would know what I'm talking about. She showed me how to see better. On the day she died, it didn't matter to her what I was wearing at the time, or what my body shape was like, or how far I could throw the softball.

I was reminded of what is truly important in life. It's not honor rolls, skin color, clothing styles, SAT scores, colleges, being number one in the state. Grandmas are more important. So are moms and dads and brothers and sisters and friends and teachers. I forget that all the time. Thank you, Nanny, as you smile from heaven, for helping me to see.

When you use your heart to see what is truly important in life, you no longer see the skin color, body shape, or social status. You no longer see the race, the religion, the societal rank. It is then that we can respect and not harass, care and not tear down, whether it is with our girlfriend, boyfriend, mom, dad, brother, sister, teacher, classmate.

I hope you'll take some risks in your life to live a little bit differently, a little bit bolder. I hope this short book has helped you to see a little bit better, to challenge you to take some risks and get out of your lawnchair. In the word's of Larry the Lawnchair Man, "You can't just sit there…not if you want to see."

I hope you hook on some weather balloons to see better, to see the goodness both in yourself and in others. And in the words of my friend Spenser Somers, I hope this book has helped you "struggle through some of the questions."

Maybe you have found some answers and maybe you are still searching. Either way, I hope you'll continue your journey to discover the goodness within.

•••••••••••

Extra Journal Pages

Joseph T. Cavanaugh

Mr. Cavanaugh has over fifteen years of experience working with youth. After graduating in 1981 from St. John's University in Collegeville, Minnesota, he became the Youth Director at Our Lady of Grace Church in Minneapolis, MN. While there, Joe developed a youth program which became one of the most active and successful in the nation. He was responsible for retreats, counseling, and staffing volunteers.

After seven years, Joe began to see the growing needs of youth in the public sector. To serve this need, in 1987 he founded Youth Frontiers, Inc., in Minneapolis. Youth Frontiers is a non-profit organization whose mission is to enrich the self-esteem of young people and to provide schools and students with direction and insight regarding ethics and relationship issues. As Executive Director, Joe provides schools with the acclaimed Oasis Retreat. During this retreat, Joe encourages, enlightens, and inspires students to learn about and discuss fundamental issues in life such as respect and compassion, fear and integrity. He has taken his exceptional motivational abilities and applied them toward other retreats, workshops, conferences, and assemblies to cover such issues as values, responsibility, sexual harassment, and young women's and young men's leadership.

Joe speaks on a national level at schools, conferences, and conventions. Along with his staff, Joe strongly believes in the mission of Youth Frontiers. By working with the youth of today, he hopes to help individuals respect and value all people.

Part of the proceeds from this book go to support Youth Frontiers, Inc. For more information about Youth Frontiers, write to:

Youth Frontiers, Inc.
1219 Marquette Avenue, Suite 80
Minneapolis, MN 55403
800 · 328 · 4827
612 · 371 · 0535

Did You Borrow This Copy?

If you would like another copy of this book for yourself or a friend, simply complete the form below and send it with your check to:

Nantucket Publications
P.O. Box 1789
Minnetonka, MN 55345

Name: _____

Address: _____

City/State/Zip: _____

Phone Number: _____

_____ *Number of copies*

_____ *x $10.99/each*

_____ *+ $2/shipping & handling*

_____ ***TOTAL***